Ding Dong!

Written by
Cath Jones

Illustrated by
Dave Cockburn

Ransom

Down at the barn,
Duck, Dog and Bird wait to be fed.

The food van zooms into the farmyard and up to the farm.

"Food!" cheer Duck, Dog and Bird.

3

The van parks in the yard.

The van man is on the porch.
He rings the bell.

Ding Dong!

Can Farmer Sam hear the bell?
No, she cannot hear the bell!

"Farmer Sam! Farmer Sam!
It's not hard to hear the bell!"
quacks Duck.

But Farmer Sam cannot hear the bell and she cannot hear Duck.

5

The van man has to go.
He has to keep the food
for Duck, Dog and Bird.

Duck, Dog and Bird are sad.
No supper for them tonight!

7

Zoom!

The van is back.
Now it has corn for the chickens.

Ding Dong! Ring Ring!

"We need to get Farmer Sam to hear the bell," quacks Duck.

Now Duck joins in!

**Ding Dong! Ring Ring!
Quack! Quack!**

But Farmer Sam cannot hear the bell.

9

"We need to get Farmer Sam to let the man in," barks Dog. "My bark is big! Farmer Sam will hear my bark."

**Ding Dong! Ring Ring!
Bark, Bark, Bark!**

But Farmer Sam cannot hear the bell.

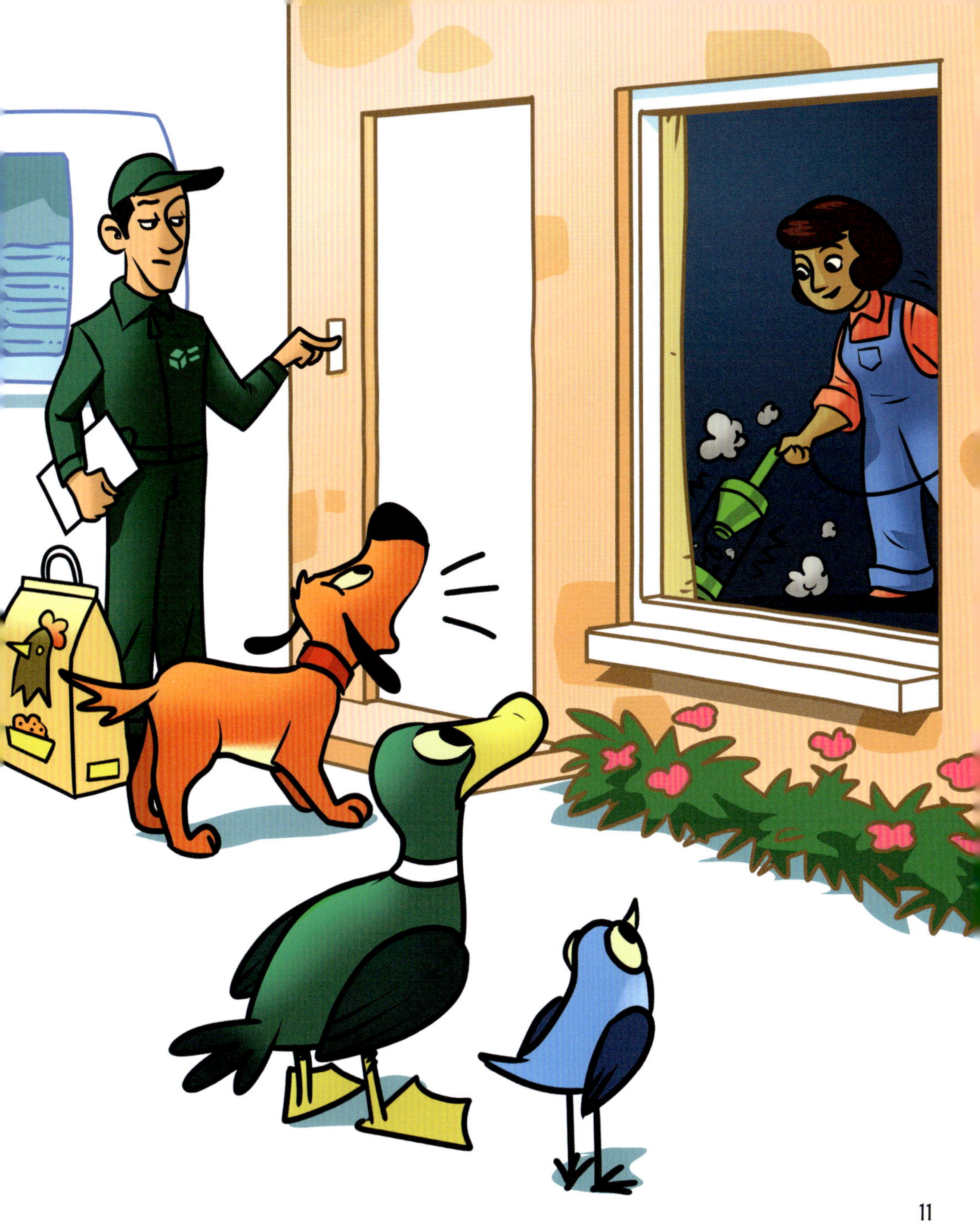

Now Bird hops up.

She tells Duck and Dog, "I will get Farmer Sam to hear."

**Ding Dong! Ring Ring!
Cheep! Cheep! Cheep!**

But it is no good.
Farmer Sam cannot hear them.

The van man has to go.
He has to keep the food
for Duck, Dog and Bird.

13

Now the van is back!

"We need to sort it **together**," Duck quacks.

The van man rings the bell. Duck, Dog and Bird sort it together.

**Ding Dong! Ring Ring!
Quack Quack Quack!
Bark, Bark, Bark!
Cheep! Cheep! Cheep!**

Yes! Farmer Sam hears them! She can get the food!

15

Now Farmer Sam has food for them all. Tonight they can get fed.

Soon they will all feel much better! Good job, Duck, Dog and Bird!